Management of Risk Pocketbook

London: TSO

information & publishing solutions

Published by TSO (The Stationery Office) and available from:

Online
www.tsoshop.co.uk

Mail, Telephone, Fax & E-mail
TSO
PO Box 29, Norwich, NR3 1GN
Telephone orders/General enquiries:
0870 600 5522
Fax orders: 0870 600 5533
E-mail: customer.services@tso.co.uk
Textphone 0870 240 3701

TSO@Blackwell and other Accredited Agents

© Crown copyright 2010

Copyright assigned to AXELOS Limited on 1st July 2013

All rights reserved. No part of this publication may be reproduced in any form or by any means without permission in writing from AXELOS Limited.

Applications to reuse, reproduce or republish material in this publication should be sent to: The Licensing Team, AXELOS Limited, Rosebery Court, St Andrews Business Park, Norwich, Norfolk NR7 0HS. Email licensing@AXELOS.com

Copyright in the typographical arrangement and design is vested in The Stationery Office Limited. Applications for reproduction should be made in writing to The Stationery Office Limited, St Crispins, Duke Street, Norwich, NR3 1PD.

The Swirl logo™ is a trade mark of AXELOS Limited

M_o_R® is a registered trade mark of AXELOS Limited

P3O® is a registered trade mark of AXELOS Limited

The AXELOS logo is a trade mark of AXELOS Limited

The Best Management Practice Official Publisher logo is a trade mark of AXELOS Limited

First edition Crown copyright 2007
Second edition Crown copyright 2010

Second impression 2013

ISBN 9780113312979 (Single copy ISBN)
ISBN 9780113312986 (Sold in a pack of 10 copies)

Printed in the United Kingdom for The Stationery Office

Material is FSC certified and produced using ECF pulp, sourced from fully sustainable forests.

P002399946   c11   11/10

Contents

Acknowledgements		**3**
1	**Introduction**	**4**
	1.1 Purpose of the guide	4
	1.2 What is a risk?	5
	1.3 What is risk management?	6
	1.4 Where and when should risk management be applied?	6
2	**Management of risk principles**	**8**
	2.1 Introduction	8
	2.2 Aligns with objectives	9
	2.3 Fits the context	10
	2.4 Engages stakeholders	10
	2.5 Provides clear guidance	11
	2.6 Informs decision-making	11
	2.7 Facilitates continual improvement	12
	2.8 Creates a supportive culture	12
	2.9 Achieves measurable value	13
3	**Management of risk approach**	**14**
	3.1 Introduction	14
	3.2 Risk management policy	15
	3.3 Risk management process guide	15
	3.4 Risk management strategy	15
	3.5 Risk register	16
	3.6 Issue register	16
	3.7 Risk improvement plan	17
	3.8 Risk communications plan	17

	3.9	Risk response plan	18
	3.10	Risk progress report	18
	3.11	Relationship between documents	18
4	**Management of risk process**	**21**
	4.1	Communicate	22
	4.2	Embed and review	22
	4.3	Identify, assess, plan, implement	22
5	**Embedding and reviewing management of risk**	**34**
	5.1	Embedding the principles	34
	5.2	Changing the culture for risk management	35
	5.3	Measuring the value	35
	5.4	Overcoming the common barriers to success	36
	5.5	Identifying and establishing opportunities for change	37
6	**Perspectives**	**38**
	6.1	Introduction	38
	6.2	Strategic perspective	40
	6.3	Programme perspective	43
	6.4	Project perspective	46
	6.5	Operational perspective	48
Glossary		**52**

Acknowledgements

OGC acknowledges, with thanks, the contribution of Graham Williams (GSW Consultancy Ltd) in the construction of this pocketbook. In addition, OGC would like to recognize the contribution of the following individuals who acted as reviewers:

Carol Bartlett, Amicar Consulting Ltd

John Fisher, Chief Examiner M_o_R, Director UnconfuseU Ltd

John Humphries, M_o_R registered consultant

1 Introduction

1.1 PURPOSE OF THE GUIDE

The *Management of Risk* (M_o_R®) guide is intended to help organizations put in place an effective framework for risk management. This will help them take informed decisions about the risks that affect their strategic, programme, project and operational objectives.

The M_o_R framework is based on four core concepts, as shown in Figure 1.1.

Figure 1.1 M_o_R framework

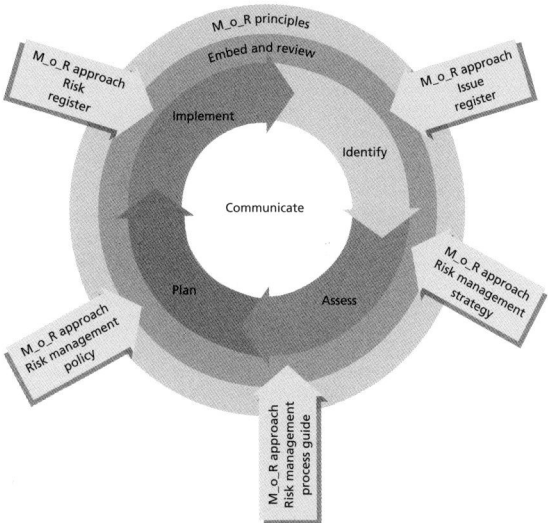

- **M_o_R principles** Principles are essential for the development and maintenance of good risk management practice. They are informed by corporate governance principles and the international standard for risk management, ISO31000: 2009. They are high-level and universally applicable statements that provide guidance to organizations as they design an appropriate approach to risk management as part of their internal controls.
- **M_o_R approach** Principles need to be adapted and adopted to suit each individual organization. An organization's approach to the principles needs to be agreed and defined within a risk management policy, process guide and strategies.
- **M_o_R process** The process is divided into four main steps: identify, assess, plan and implement. Each step describes the inputs, outputs, tasks and techniques involved to ensure that the overall process is effective.
- **Embedding and reviewing M_o_R** Having put in place an approach and process that satisfies the principles, an organization should ensure that they are consistently applied across the organization and that their application undergoes continual improvement in order for them to be effective.

1.2 WHAT IS A RISK?

Risk *is defined as 'an uncertain event or set of events that, should it occur, will have an effect on the achievement of objectives. A risk is measured by the combination of the probability of a perceived threat or opportunity occurring and the magnitude of its impact on objectives.'*

All organizations, including temporary ones such as those concerned with programmes or projects, will encounter uncertain events when trying to achieve their objectives. These uncertain events may arise inside or outside the organization. Each individual uncertain event that would impact one or more objectives is known as a risk. Within this definition, 'threat' is used to describe an uncertain event that would have a negative impact on objectives if it occurred and 'opportunity' is used to describe an uncertain event that would have a positive impact on objectives if it occurred. The combined effect of risks to a set of objectives is known as risk exposure, and is the extent of the risk borne by that part of the organization at that time.

1.3 WHAT IS RISK MANAGEMENT?

The term '**risk management**' refers to the systematic application of principles, an approach and a process to the tasks of identifying and assessing risks, and then planning and implementing risk responses. This provides a disciplined environment for proactive decision-making.

For risk management to be effective, risks need to be identified, assessed and controlled.

1.4 WHERE AND WHEN SHOULD RISK MANAGEMENT BE APPLIED?

Risk management should be applied continuously with information made available when critical decisions are being made. Decisions about risk will vary depending on whether the risk relates to long-, medium- or short-term organizational objectives (see Figure 1.2).

- **Strategic** decisions are primarily concerned with long-term goals; these set the context for decisions at other levels of the organization. The risks associated with strategic decisions

may not become apparent until well into the future. It is, therefore, essential to review these decisions and associated risks regularly.
- Medium-term goals are usually addressed through **programmes** and **projects** to bring about business change. Decisions relating to medium-term goals are narrower in scope than strategic ones, particularly in terms of timeframe and financial responsibilities.
- At the **operational** level, the emphasis is on short-term goals to ensure ongoing continuity of business services. Decisions about risk at this level, however, must also support the achievement of long- and medium-term goals.

Figure 1.2 Organizational perspectives

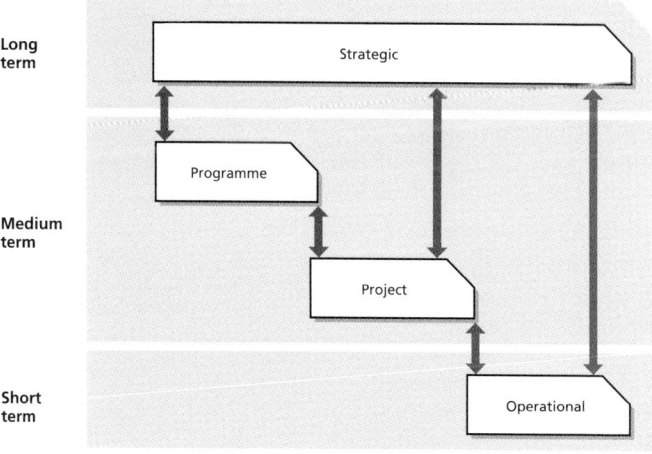

2 Management of risk principles

2.1 INTRODUCTION

The *Management of Risk* (M_o_R) guide provides a framework for risk management that can be applied to any organization regardless of its size, complexity, location, or the sector within which it operates. This is possible because M_o_R is principles-based. Principles are characterized as:

- Universal in that they apply to every organization
- Self-validating in that they have been proven in practice over many years
- Empowering because they give risk practitioners added confidence and ability to influence and shape risk management across the organization.

The M_o_R principles are informed by corporate governance principles and the international standard for risk management ISO31000: 2009. They are intended to guide rather than dictate so that organizations can develop their own policies, process, strategies and plans to meet their specific needs.

Effective risk management satisfies the following eight principles:

- Aligns with objectives
- Fits the context
- Engages stakeholders
- Provides clear guidance
- Informs decision-making
- Facilitates continual improvement
- Creates a supportive culture
- Achieves measurable value.

The first seven principles are enablers. The final principle is the result of implementing risk management well. For risk management to become more than a compliance-led activity within an organization, the value of risk management, measured by the return on investment of risk management work, must be determined and communicated.

To remain competitive in a changing and uncertain world, organizations need to learn and adapt. Not all organizations will need the same arrangements to manage risk. The context, size, extent of operations and services and the inherent uncertainty in the work being undertaken will shape actual practices. The M_o_R principles provide the foundation from which scalable and context specific practices can be developed and continually refined to support organizational performance. Together, the eight principles form a coherent whole to ensure successful risk management.

2.2 ALIGNS WITH OBJECTIVES

> Risk management aligns continually with organizational objectives.

Many situations are uncertain, but risk management is focused only on those uncertainties that have the potential to impact the achievement of one or more objectives of the organization. As a result, organizations must pay close attention to understanding objectives so that an appropriate balance can be achieved between maximizing opportunities and minimizing threats.

2.3 FITS THE CONTEXT

> Risk management is designed to fit the current context.

Satisfying this principle relies on the bespoke design of the risk management approach to match the current context. This relies on a thorough understanding of the external and internal context, how it is changing and the pace of any change. For the organization as a whole the external context will include the sector, markets, locations, technologies and regulatory regimes that provide the backdrop for organizational performance. The internal context includes the culture, formal and informal structures, relationships between stakeholders and processes deployed.

2.4 ENGAGES STAKEHOLDERS

> Risk management engages stakeholders and deals with differing perceptions of risk.

Most organizations have large numbers of disparate stakeholders, some within and some outside the organization. Stakeholders play a wide range of roles, including providing funding, approvals, requirements definition, design, information and advice. Engaging stakeholders requires the adoption of an appropriate level and style of communication in order to identify those individuals and groups who have a stake in the organizational activity being undertaken, to understand their requirements and perceptions of risk, and to influence their contribution.

2.5 PROVIDES CLEAR GUIDANCE

> Risk management provides clear and coherent guidance to stakeholders.

Risk management practices must be clear to ensure that stakeholders, including clients, partners, suppliers, regulators, decision-makers and staff, can see how the organization identifies, assesses and controls risks to objectives across multiple perspectives. In addition to being clear, it is important that risk practices integrate to form a coherent approach across the various units and activities that make up the organization. Coherent practices are logical, orderly and consistent.

2.6 INFORMS DECISION-MAKING

> Risk management is linked to and informs decision-making across the organization.

Decisions in organizations are necessarily taken when some factors that may impact the outcome are uncertain and pose a risk to objectives being achieved. Given that risks influence every decision, risk management must help decision-makers understand the relative merits, threats and opportunities associated with alternative courses of action and make informed choices. One way that risk management enables effective decision-making is by resourcing risk management to establish transparent roles, responsibilities, reporting and escalation arrangements.

2.7 FACILITATES CONTINUAL IMPROVEMENT

> Risk management uses historical data and facilitates learning and continual improvement.

There are a number of ways in which risk management facilitates continual improvement within the organization. Collecting actual performance data, including information about risks that were identified, assessed and controlled (or not), means that new organizational activities have history and experience to draw upon to inform estimates, risk responses, forecasts and decisions.

2.8 CREATES A SUPPORTIVE CULTURE

> Risk management creates a culture that recognizes uncertainty and supports considered risk-taking.

Culture is understood here to mean 'the way things are done'. For risk management to add value, an organizational culture must be created which recognizes that to manage risk appropriately means taking calculated chances. Zero risk is neither possible, nor desirable, and a tolerable level of risk that matches the appetite for the organizational activity is needed. An effective organization creates a supportive culture where wins and losses are understood and are treated as opportunities for improvement.

2.9 ACHIEVES MEASURABLE VALUE

> Risk management enables achievement of measurable organizational value.

At the heart of risk management is the assertion summed up by the proverb 'prevention is better than cure'. This asserts that it costs less to anticipate and manage a potential risk than it does to recover from an actual issue that is affecting objectives. With respect to opportunities, the business case for proactive identification, assessment and control is to ensure that positive risks are spotted and seized, rather than being allowed to drift by with the organization unable to capitalize on them. In short, investments in risk management are expected to provide a tangible return for the organization.

3 Management of risk approach

3.1 INTRODUCTION

The way in which the principles are implemented will vary from organization to organization. Collectively the principles provide a foundation from which the risk management approach for an organization can be developed. This chapter describes the M_o_R approach. An organization can adapt this approach to meet its specific needs and objectives.

Central to the M_o_R approach is the creation of a set of documentation comprising:

- Risk management policy
- Risk management process guide
- Risk management strategies for each organizational activity.

The policy, process guide and strategies provide the explanation of how the organization will implement risk management. They describe the activities to be undertaken, the sequence in which these are carried out, and the roles and responsibilities necessary for their delivery.

In support of the risk management policy, process guide and strategies, the M_o_R approach also recommends the use of other documents. These documents fall into three categories – records, plans and reports – as listed below:

- Records
    - Risk register
    - Issue register
- Plans
    - Risk improvement plan
    - Risk communications plan

- Risk response plan
- Reports
  - Risk progress report.

3.2 RISK MANAGEMENT POLICY

Describes why risk management is important to the organization, and the specific objectives served by implementing a formal risk management approach.

The policy is the method of communicating, in a common language, why risk management should be undertaken and how it relates to the corporate objectives. The policy strives to accomplish uniformity across risk management processes and it aims to remove ambiguity about the organization's overall risk capacity, appetite and tolerance levels. It also describes the format, timing and content of reports.

3.3 RISK MANAGEMENT PROCESS GUIDE

Describes how an organization intends to carry out risk management and the role and responsibility of people who perform risk management related tasks.

It describes how the M_o_R process steps of identify, assess, plan and implement will be carried out in the organization. It should be designed for the organization and be suitable for all types of activity across the organization.

3.4 RISK MANAGEMENT STRATEGY

Documents the way the risk management policy and process will be implemented for a specific organizational activity.

It would be typical for multiple strategies to be prepared – one for each distinct organizational activity, for example, a specific change programme or project, a specific operational area, or a specific cross-organizational initiative. The key guidance is that strategies must be specific to the organizational activity, while at the same time reflecting the overall organizational policy document(s) and process guide. The risk management strategy is the document that will outline the risk appetite for an activity. Risk appetite is expressed using risk tolerance thresholds and these are defined through activity specific probability and impact scales for each objective. A risk management strategy should be established when planning any organizational activity and be implemented before the work starts.

3.5 RISK REGISTER

Documents all of the risks that have been identified as having an impact on the objectives of the organizational activity.

The risk register, at any point in time, should provide a snapshot of the identified risks for the organizational activity in question, the priority of each of the risks, the risk owner for each risk, and the response strategy chosen by each risk owner. The risk register should also record when the risk was closed and why. In addition to the risk register, risk responses may be further elaborated and reported in a risk response plan.

3.6 ISSUE REGISTER

Documents all of the unplanned situations that are happening now and that require management attention. Issues could be problems, benefits, queries or change requests.

Although issue resolution is not part of the risk management process, the issue register is the link between these two processes. Issues may have arisen from risks that had been identified, but not managed. Issues that have been raised may be causes of new risks. It is, therefore, important to understand issues and how they are related to, yet different from, risks.

3.7 RISK IMPROVEMENT PLAN

Brings together all the actions required to improve the way that risk management is performed by the organization, or a subset of it. It includes, but is not limited to, improving the culture and context within which risk management process can add value.

It provides a record of the current 'health' and/or maturity of risk management within the organization, the targets that have been set, the time period within which it is planned targets will be achieved, and the planned mechanisms/methods that will be used to achieve the desired changes.

3.8 RISK COMMUNICATIONS PLAN

Describes how information will be disseminated to, and received from, all relevant stakeholders of a particular organizational activity. This may be a separate document or part of a wider communications plan for the organizational activity in question.

Effective communication between stakeholders is a critical success factor for risk management, to ensure that context is understood, risks are identified and assessed, and suitable responses planned and owned. As with all communications plans, two-way communication is essential, so the plan must outline processes for handling feedback as well as information about the messages to be transmitted.

3.9 RISK RESPONSE PLAN

The risk response plan, when used, is linked to the risk response field of the risk register. Its purpose is to detail specific plans for responding to a single or linked set of risks. Such a document is useful where a particular risk event or group of related risk events warrants a significant and resource-intensive response(s). It is also useful as a way of providing information to risk owners and actionees, and for tracking progress against planned actions.

3.10 RISK PROGRESS REPORT

The purpose of the risk progress report is to provide regular progress information to management on risk management within a particular organizational activity. It may be a separate document, or may form part of a wider progress report.

A risk progress report will comment on the progress of planned actions and the effectiveness of these. It will also report trend analysis and report performance against measures established to demonstrate the value of risk management activities.

3.11 RELATIONSHIP BETWEEN DOCUMENTS

The documents that constitute the M_o_R approach are clearly connected as shown in Figure 3.1.

Figure 3.1 shows the linkages between the documents that make up the M_o_R approach for one organizational activity. Multiple instances of each type of document are likely to exist in a larger organization as they reflect specific policy, process and strategy for different organizational perspectives. The relationships between the documents however remain constant so that the M_o_R approach within each distinct organizational activity is coherent, and is a subset of the desired organizational approach to risk management.

Figure 3.1 Relationship between documents

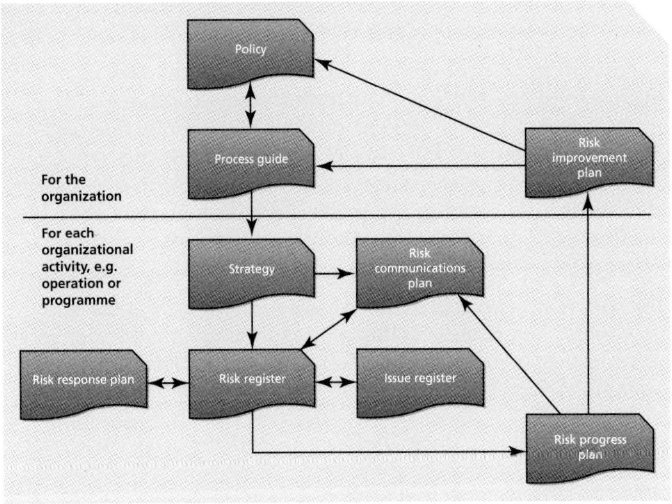

At an organizational level, a risk management policy, a risk management process guide and at least one risk management strategy must exist. These documents will make it clear where other subsets of the organization may establish their own modified approach to meet the specific needs of its objectives, context and stakeholders.

The risk register and issue register are different documents with a different purpose but are clearly linked. Where risk response plans are used, configuration control between these and the risk register for that activity must be maintained continually.

Multiple risk and issue registers will exist within an organization and a way of ensuring that risks and issues are handled within the correct perspective is essential.

The risk improvement plan has close links with the M_o_R approach (policy, process guide and strategy) for the organizational activity in question, and the organization as a whole. Improvements must be coordinated across the organization, with clear reporting of plans and progress, via the risk progress report. Risk progress reports may be separate documents or part of wider activity level progress reports, e.g. for a programme, project or operational activity.

Risk communications plans are needed for each organizational activity but again need linking with reporting between activities and each organizational perspective as well as with wider communications plans.

4 Management of risk process

The overall management of risk process is illustrated in Figure 4.1. The steps are represented as a circle of arrows, as it is common for the entire process to be completed several times in the lifecycle of an organizational activity.

Figure 4.1 The management of risk process

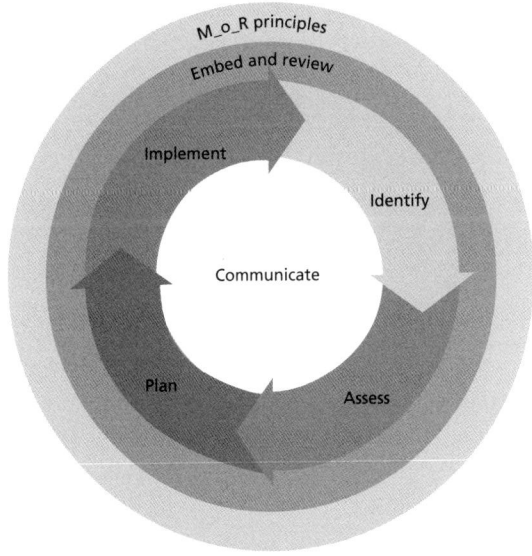

4.1 COMMUNICATE

The 'communicate' activity deliberately stands alone, as the findings of any individual step may be communicated to management for action prior to the completion of the overall process. Rather than being a distinct stage in the M_o_R process, communication is an activity that is carried out throughout the whole process.

A number of aspects of communication should be recognized and addressed if risk management is to be effective. An organization's exposure to risk is never static: effective communication is key to the identification of new threats and opportunities or changes in existing risks. The implementation of risk management is dependent on participation, and participation, in turn, is dependent on communication.

4.2 EMBED AND REVIEW

'Embed and review' embraces all of the steps in the process as this activity looks at each individual step in turn to determine its contribution to the overall effectiveness of the complete process. The M_o_R principles form the foundation for all risk management activities and permeate all risk management process steps.

4.3 IDENTIFY, ASSESS, PLAN, IMPLEMENT

The M_o_R process is divided into four further primary process steps known as:

- Identify
- Assess
- Plan
- Implement.

Collectively these steps form a logical sequence necessary for robust implementation of risk management. They are carried out in sequence, as any one step cannot be undertaken until the preceding step has been completed. They are all repetitive in nature in that when additional information becomes available, it is often necessary to revisit earlier steps and carry them out again, to achieve a complete picture of the risks to the activity at that time.

A simple process map for each step is shown in Figure 4.2, and this illustrates the types of information movement. These types of data movement are used to describe how the management of risk steps are implemented, and how the output of one process step forms the input to the subsequent process step.

Figure 4.2 How each process step is defined

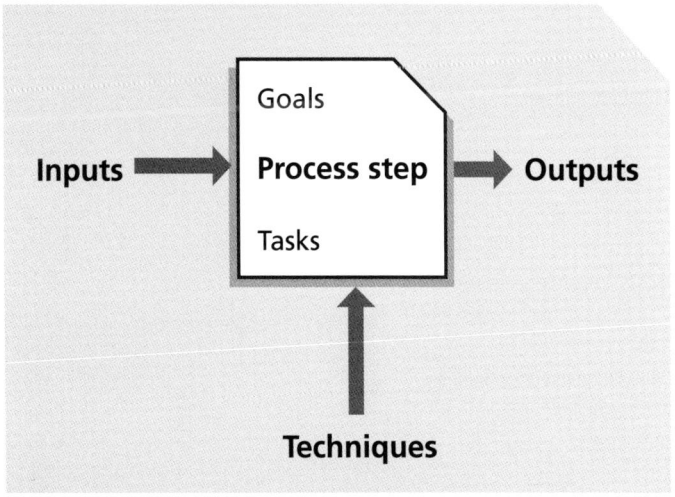

4.3.1 Identify

The identify process step is further divided into the following steps:

- Context
- Identify the risks.

Context

The goal of identify – context is to obtain information about the planned activity and how it fits into the wider organization and market/society (e.g. activity objectives and scope, assumptions and constraints, stakeholders and where the activity fits in relation to the organizational structure). It is within this step that the risk management strategy for the organizational activity is created and/or updated.

Figure 4.3 The context process step: definition and information flows

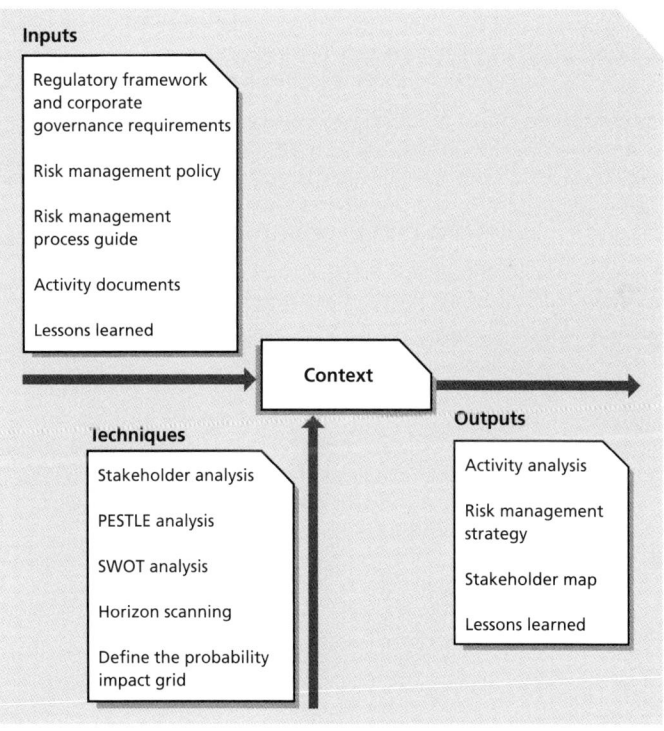

Identify the risks

The goal of identify – identify the risks is to identify risks to the activity objectives with the aim of minimizing threats whilst maximizing opportunities. This will include preparing a risk register, preparing key performance indicators and early warning indicators, and understanding the stakeholders' view of the risks.

Identified risks must be described in a way so that they can be understood by stakeholders who read the description after the risks have been entered into the risk register. The accepted form for risk descriptions is to create a risk 'string' that separates causes from risk events and from effects.

A useful and commonly accepted way of expressing risk is to consider the following aspect of each risk:

- **Risk cause** Describes the source of the risk, i.e. the event or situation that gives rise to the risk. These are often referred to as risk drivers. They are not risks in themselves, but the potential trigger points for risk. These may be either internal or external to the organizational activity under consideration.
- **Risk event** Describes the area of uncertainty in terms of the threat or the opportunity (using may or might in this part of the description is helpful).
- **Risk effect** Describes the impact that the risk would have on the organizational activity should the risk materialize.

Figure 4.4 The identify the risks process step: definition and information flows

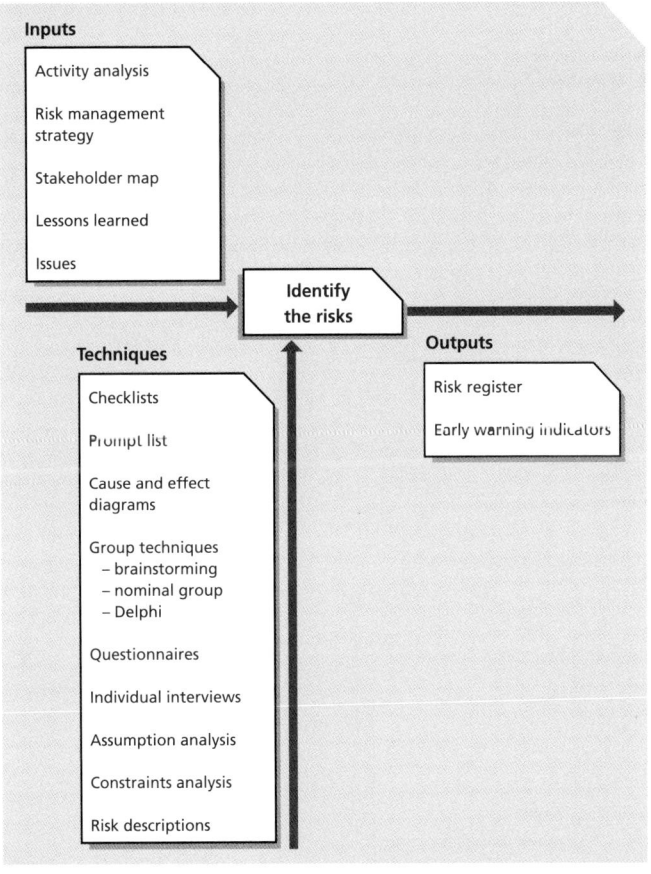

4.3.2 Assess

The assess process step is further divided into the following steps:

- Estimate
- Evaluate.

Estimate

The goal of assess – estimate is to prioritize individual risks so that it is clear which risks are most important and most urgent. This will require an understanding of the probability (How likely is it to occur?), the impact (What would be the effect on activity objectives?) and the proximity (When would the risk occur if it did?) of each threat and opportunity.

Figure 4.5 The estimate process step: definition and information flows

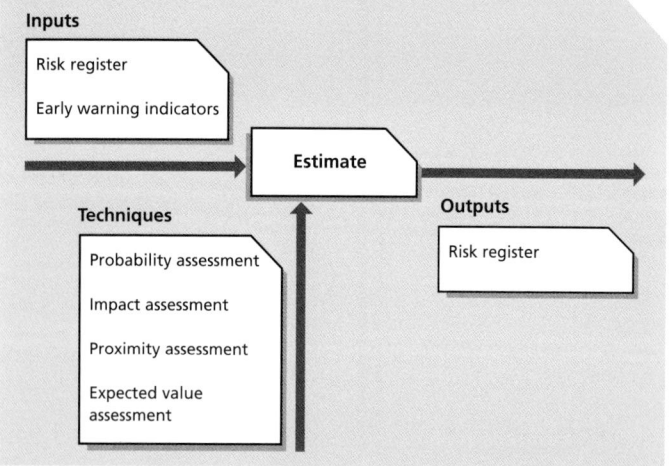

Evaluate

The goal of assess – evaluate is to understand the risk exposure faced by the activity by looking at the net effect of the identified threats and opportunities on an activity when aggregated together.

Figure 4.6 The evaluate process step: definition and information flows

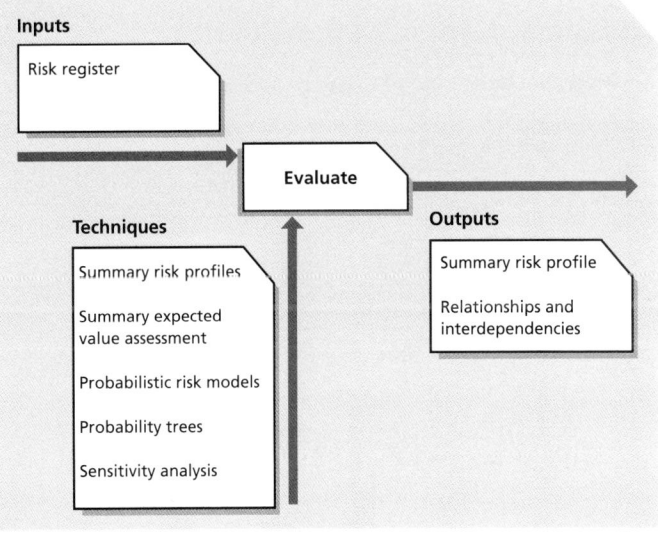

4.3.3 Plan

The goal of plan is to prepare specific management responses to the threats and opportunities identified ideally to remove or reduce the threats and to maximize the opportunities. Attention to this step ensures as far as possible that the business and its staff are not taken by surprise if a risk materializes.

Figure 4.7 The plan process step: definition and information flows

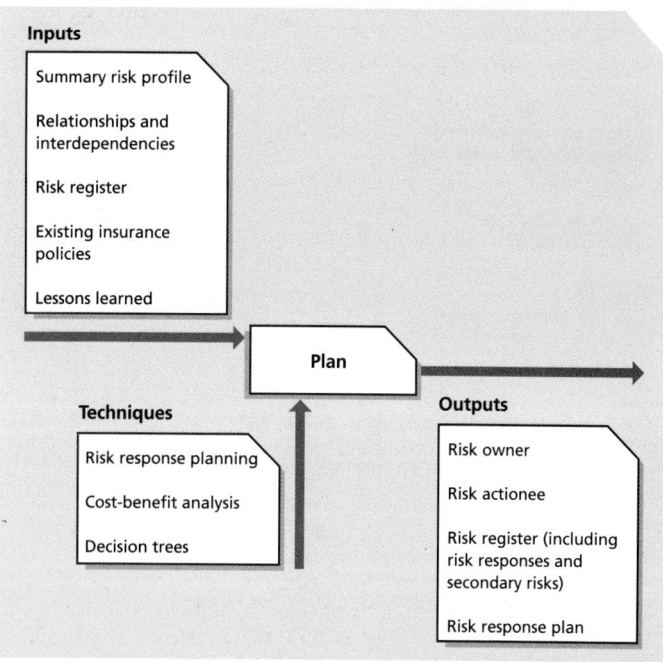

Risk response planning

Risks that are important and/or urgent enough to warrant investment in action must be responded to in the optimal way. Risk response planning enables a range of response strategies to be considered, and the approach that provides the maximum change to the risk exposure (combined probability and impact) for the least investment is chosen. Table 4.1 shows the generic risk response types that are available for threats and opportunities with an explanation of when each is useful.

Table 4.1 Generic risk response options

Response options	Use
Avoid a threat Exploit an opportunity	This option is about making the uncertain situation certain by removing the risk. This can often be achieved by removing the cause of a threat, or by implementing the cause of an opportunity.
Reduce a threat Enhance an opportunity	This option chooses definite action now to change the probability and/or the impact of the risk. The term mitigate is relevant when discussing reduction of a threat, i.e. making the threat less likely to occur and/or reducing the impact if it did.
Transfer the risk	Transfer is an option that aims to pass part of the risk to a third party. Insurance is the classic form of transfer, where the insurer picks up the risk cost, but the insured retains the impact on other objectives, e.g. time delay. Transfer can apply to opportunities, where a third party gains a cost benefit but the primary risk taker gains another benefit.

Share the risk	Share is an option that is different in nature from the transfer response. It seeks for multiple parties, typically within a supply chain, to share the risk on a pain/gain share basis.
Accept the risk	The accept option means that the organization 'takes the chance' that the risk will occur, with its full impact if it did. There is no change to residual risk with the accept option, but neither are any costs incurred now to manage the risk, or to prepare to manage the risk in future.
Prepare contingent plans	This option involves preparing plans now, but not taking action now. Most usually associated with the accept option, preparing contingent plans in this instance is saying: 'We will accept the risk for now, but we'll make a plan for what we'll do if the situation changes.' This option applies equally to other responses and is often referred to as a 'fallback' plan, i.e. what we will do if the original response doesn't work. Fallback plans apply to all other strategies, even avoiding a threat and exploiting an opportunity, because the plan to avoid/exploit may not be successful despite good intentions.

4.3.4 Implement

The goal of implement is to ensure that the planned risk management actions are implemented and monitored as to their effectiveness, and corrective action is taken where responses do not match expectations.

Figure 4.8 The implement process step: definition and information flows

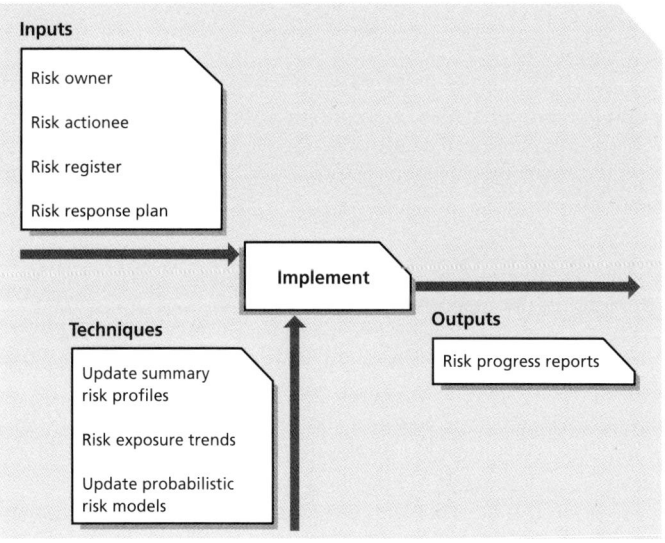

5 Embedding and reviewing management of risk

How an organization manages risk is an expression of its core values and communicates to stakeholders its appetite for and attitude to risk-taking. A disconnected or unmanaged approach to risk management is more likely to lead to reactive rather than proactive management where unforeseen issues are commonplace. Such a situation can leave stakeholders feeling less confident about the organization's ability to manage its affairs appropriately. It is important therefore to embed risk management into the culture and to put in place mechanisms to review and confirm that the approach to risk management remains appropriate given the organization's objectives and context.

5.1 EMBEDDING THE PRINCIPLES

Embedding risk management into an organization must start with the M_o_R principles and an appreciation of what the organization would look and feel like should the principles be embedded into the culture.

What would an organization be like where these principles were a natural part of the way that work was done across the strategic, programme, project and operational perspectives? Answering this question and developing measures against which to review and evaluate the degree to which risk management is integrated into the culture is a necessary step.

5.2 CHANGING THE CULTURE FOR RISK MANAGEMENT

Bringing about cultural change is no easy task for any organization. Often smaller organizations can achieve better results, more quickly. Quite often the same individual undertakes multiple roles and has several responsibilities associated with the management of risk, which can result in a better understanding and a more influential mandate for change. Also, within a small organization fewer participants are typically involved overall. Within large organizations the management of risk roles and responsibilities tend to be dispersed, resulting in a need for more complex integration and communication.

Whatever the size of the organization, the M_o_R approach (policy, process guide and strategy) and associated records, plans and reports provide the documented commitment to risk management. But to change the culture, these documents need to be understood, valued, implemented and improved by staff across the organization and this is no small task.

5.3 MEASURING THE VALUE

A number of indicators can be used to judge the success of efforts to build a risk management culture. These include:

- Questionnaires to collect information relating to the organization, its business, people and activities
- Benchmarks to measure the impact that a risk management awareness programme has in an organization, or the level of impact that introducing fresh or new risk management practices has
- Sampling understanding and knowledge within the staff via questionnaires to measure the benefits from an education, training or awareness programme.

5.4 OVERCOMING THE COMMON BARRIERS TO SUCCESS

There are a number of barriers or constraints common to the implementation of all the steps in the risk management process. Some of the barriers are described below:

- Lack of an organizational culture that appreciates the benefits of risk management
- Immature risk management practices
- Lack of risk facilitation resources and time
- Lack of policies, processes, strategies and plans
- Lack of a senior management sponsorship
- Lack of training, knowledge and formal risk tools and techniques
- Lack of clear guidance for managers and staff
- Lack of incentives for participation in risk management activities.

A clear demonstration of sponsorship, responsibility and endorsement from the person at board level with responsibility for understanding and managing risk is necessary to ensure that risk management is taken seriously, given the priority it deserves and embraced within the organization.

The board has ultimate responsibility for risk management and relies on others, such as senior management and middle management, for:

- The creation of a management infrastructure to ensure that risk is managed and integrated across the whole business
- The inclusion of risk management in job descriptions, the setting of performance objectives aligned to the framework and the inclusion of risk in the appraisals process for all staff.

5.5 IDENTIFYING AND ESTABLISHING OPPORTUNITIES FOR CHANGE

Organizations should identify opportunities to emphasize their support and commitment to risk management, deliver key messages, and check that risk management is taking place appropriately.

Trigger points should also be used to monitor and review risks and decisions made on those risks, thereby establishing a continual cycle of monitoring, review and update/improvement. This will help to ensure that risk-based decisions remain appropriate and informed as the organization changes or its objectives change.

6 Perspectives

6.1 INTRODUCTION

The way in which the principles, approach and process are applied will vary according to the nature of the context within which they are being carried out.

Within any organization, the various contexts will lie somewhere on a continuum between:

- Maintaining the status quo through day-to-day management of the organization's product or service delivery, and
- Establishing the future direction for the organization and moving the organization in that direction by means of change management.

Within the M_o_R guide, the various contexts are described from different organizational perspectives. The organizational perspectives considered can be briefly described as:

- **Strategic** Concerned with ensuring overall business success, vitality and viability
- **Programme** Concerned with transforming business strategy into new ways of working that deliver measurable benefits to the organization
- **Project** Concerned with delivering defined outputs to an appropriate level of quality within agreed scope, time and cost constraints
- **Operational** Concerned with maintaining appropriate levels of business services to existing and new customers.

Although these perspectives are described individually, there are important relationships that need to be established and maintained between these organizational perspectives for risk management to be effective. The interrelationships between these perspectives are shown in Figure 6.1.

Figure 6.1 Interrelationships between different organizational perspectives

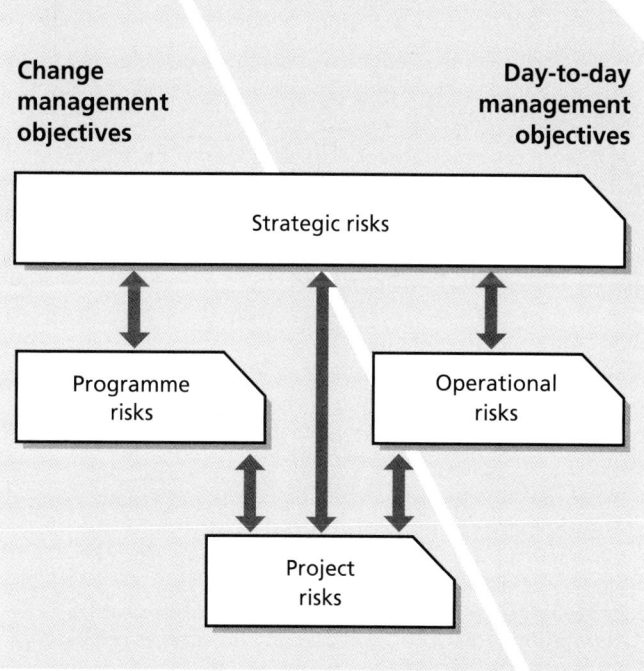

In addition to the application of risk management to each perspective, an organization needs to integrate risk management activities across the entire portfolio of work that is being undertaken. The term 'enterprise risk management' (ERM) is often used to describe this activity. It seeks to understand the relationships between risks across the strategic, programme, project and operational perspectives and from multiple risk specialist viewpoints. Information collated through ERM is used to determine the optimal blend of responses to risks whether that is through financial provisions or non-financial methods.

ERM activities can be managed in a portfolio office as described in OGC guidance on *Portfolio, Programme and Project Offices* (P3O®) (TSO, 2008).

Guidance on the application of risk management principles where portfolio management has been adopted is described in the OGC guide *Management of Portfolios* (MoP™) (TSO, 2011).

6.2 STRATEGIC PERSPECTIVE

6.2.1 Aligns with objectives

The strategic perspective is principally concerned with achieving desired outcomes by defending or changing organizational performance. Strategic objectives will generally consist of a mixture of the following types of objectives:

- **Financial** Relating to tangible measures that satisfy stakeholder or shareholder expectations
- **Core service** Tending to relate to increasing efficiency, quality or output
- **Stakeholder or customer** Relating to ensuring that reputation is managed and demand for services remains strong and predictable

- **Organizational capability** Relating to ensuring that the organization remains relevant and able to meet future needs (e.g. innovation and new service development)
- **Resource** Relating to ensuring that staff and suppliers are providing the skills and commodities required by the organization.

It is critical that risk management within the strategic perspective is continually aligned with objectives, i.e. that the processes used to set and re-confirm strategic objectives are dynamic and adaptive.

6.2.2 Fits the context

The strategic perspective maintains a view of executive-level decision-making relative to the organization's external environment and to other organizations that work with or against it.

6.2.3 Engages stakeholders

Strategic stakeholders are likely to include those drawn from the following groups: owners or shareholders, investors or funders; key customers or customer groups; political, legal or regulatory bodies; trade unions or other staff representatives; the wider community in which the affected organization exists; strategic partners or suppliers; and employees.

6.2.4 Provides clear guidance

Risk management for the strategic perspective should be shaped by the risk management policy and process guide and is documented in the strategic risk management strategy.

The risk management strategy for the strategic perspective will define how management of risk will be handled by the accounting officer/chief executive officer (CEO), executive management team and management board.

6.2.5 Informs decision-making

Decisions informed by risk management at the strategic level represent the most fundamental choices made by senior management and other key decision-making stakeholders. These will include choices about the products and/or services undertaken, the markets and sectors served, how funding is secured, numbers of staff, underpinning values etc.

Strategic risks that exceed tolerances set by the accounting officer/CEO are very serious as they will have a significant impact on the proper functioning of the organization and may even affect its survival. These risks require prompt reporting to the accounting officer/CEO. Strategic risks should be escalated to the management board when they exceed the risk tolerance set for the organization within the strategic risk management strategy.

6.2.6 Facilitates continual improvement

When making a new corporate investment decision or beginning a new corporate planning cycle, the full risk management process should be applied. A key output from earlier steps will be the strategic risk management strategy, which will define how the management of risk will be handled as part of the current strategic planning cycle or investment decision. As risks are identified and assessed, information will be captured in the strategic risk register together with the planned risk responses once these are agreed.

At the end of each business planning cycle, the strategic risk management strategy and its implementation should be reviewed for its effectiveness and lessons learned. As part of this process, a strategic level risk improvement plan could be prepared. During subsequent business planning cycles, the risk process should be repeated but lessons learned from earlier iterations should be incorporated.

6.2.7 Creates a supportive culture

Application of this principle requires senior managers to demonstrate through their words and actions that risk management is important to the organization. Creating a supportive culture requires senior leaders to acknowledge risk and to encourage people to uncover risky areas of the organization and do something about them.

6.3 PROGRAMME PERSPECTIVE

6.3.1 Aligns with objectives

Programme objectives are principally concerned with achieving desired outcomes in the form of step change improvements to organizational performance. Programme objectives will consist of a mixture of the following types of objectives:

- **Benefits** Relating to some form of measurable improvement that is deemed of value by a stakeholder. These objectives may be linked to strategic level key performance indicators where possible. Benefit objectives may be tangible or intangible. Benefit objectives may be expressed in financial or non-financial terms depending on the nature of the benefit.

- **Capability** Relating to a business change that develops a new capability, enhances an existing capability, or removes a capability that is no longer desired. Capability objectives will affect the operational performance of the organization. These objectives should be mapped to projects within the programme that deliver the change.

6.3.2 Fits the context

The programme perspective maintains a view of a significant change to the organization relative to other changes and the ongoing operations of the organization.

6.3.3 Engages stakeholders

Programme stakeholders are likely to include those drawn from the following groups: owners or shareholders, executive management, operational management, and the staff of the organization; customers or consumers who will be affected by the programme's outcome; internal and/or external audit; trade unions or other staff representatives; political or regulatory bodies; the wider community in which the affected organization exists; project management teams delivering the projects within the programme; and the programme management team.

6.3.4 Provides clear guidance

Risk management for the programme perspective should be shaped by the risk management policy and process guide and is documented in the programme risk management strategy.

The risk management strategy for the programme perspective will define how the senior responsible owner, programme manager and programme board will handle the management of risk.

6.3.5 Informs decision-making

Regular programme risk reports should be provided to the senior responsible owner and programme manager. Additional summary risk reports (e.g. risk progress reports) may be produced at key decision points such as at the end of programme definition and at the end of each tranche of the programme.

If individual programme risks or the overall programme risk exposure exceed the tolerances set these risks require prompt reporting to the senior responsible owner and programme board. They will escalate to the strategic perspective if the level of risk cannot be brought under control.

6.3.6 Facilitates continual improvement

For a new programme, the risk management process should commence at the outset with key risks captured as part of the programme brief. During programme definition, the full process should be applied with a key output being a programme risk management strategy that defines how the management of risk will be handled during the lifetime of the programme. As risks are identified and assessed, this information will be captured in the programme risk register together with the planned risk responses once these are agreed.

At the end of each tranche, the programme risk management strategy should be reviewed for its effectiveness, lessons learned should be documented, and the full risk process should be repeated incorporating lessons learned from earlier iterations.

6.3.7 Creates a supportive culture

The programme manager and senior responsible owner have a key role to play in creating a supportive culture for risk management for the programme. If they show through their words and actions that risk management is important, others will follow.

6.4 PROJECT PERSPECTIVE

6.4.1 Aligns with objectives

The objectives of project risk management are to inform decision-making during project selection and definition and to improve project performance during design and delivery so that completed projects lead to enhanced organizational performance. A project exists to deliver a set of business products in accordance with an agreed business case. The objectives of the project that risk management is focused on therefore will be the delivery of those business products and their associated benefits:

- To specification
- On time
- Within budget.

6.4.2 Fits the context

The project perspective maintains a view of successfully delivering a predefined output or product and, as a consequence, enabling the delivery of business benefits to the organization.

6.4.3 Engages stakeholders with differing perceptions of risk

Project stakeholders are likely to include those drawn from the following groups: internal and external suppliers; customers or recipients of project deliverables; political or regulatory bodies; trade unions or other staff representatives; project sponsors; project management; and team members.

6.4.4 Provides clear guidance

Risk management for the project perspective should be shaped by the risk management policy and process guide and is documented in the project risk management strategy. It may also be influenced by the programme risk management strategy where the project forms part of a programme.

The risk management strategy for the project perspective will define how the project senior responsible owner, project manager and project board will manage risk over the lifetime of the project.

6.4.5 Informs decision-making

Project risk progress reports should be provided by the project manager at key decision points, for example at project stage/decision gates.

If individual project risks or the overall project risk exposure exceed the tolerances set, these risks require prompt reporting to the senior responsible owner and project board. They will escalate to the programme perspective if the level of risk cannot be brought under control and the project is part of a programme or to the strategic perspective if the project is not being managed as part of a wider programme.

6.4.6 Facilitates continual improvement

For a new project, the risk management process should commence at the outset with key risks captured as part of the start-up process. During project initiation, the full process should be applied and a key output will be a project risk management strategy that defines how the management of risk will be handled during the lifetime of the project. As risks are identified and assessed, this information will be captured in the project risk register together with the planned risk responses once these are agreed.

At the end of each stage, the project risk management strategy should be reviewed for its effectiveness, lessons learned should be documented, and the full risk process should be repeated incorporating lessons learned from earlier iterations.

6.4.7 Creates a supportive culture

The senior responsible owner, project manager and project board have a key role to play in creating a supportive culture for risk management for the project. If they show through their words and actions that risk management is important, others will follow.

6.5 OPERATIONAL PERSPECTIVE

6.5.1 Aligns with objectives

Operational objectives are concerned with the successful day-to-day management of the organization. Objectives generally relate to specific levels of service delivery performance and improvements to organizational performance. Operational objectives may therefore consider:

- Reputation of the specific operational area
- Volume (e.g. customers or units produced)
- Cost (e.g. per unit produced)
- Quality (e.g. unit or process failures)
- Internal control (e.g. health, safety or failure)
- Revenue
- Staff (e.g. satisfaction)
- Customer (e.g. churn, satisfaction).

6.5.2 Fits the context

The operational perspective maintains a view of the people, processes and technologies that support ongoing business-as-usual or service delivery activities of the organization in relation to customer expectations. In this context, services may be delivered to internal customers (e.g. by a human resources function) or to external customers (e.g. financial management services by a money management firm). The operational perspective also monitors how strategic changes to the organization affect ongoing business-as-usual and service delivery activities.

6.5.3 Engages stakeholders

Operational stakeholders are likely to include those drawn from the following groups: owners or shareholders, executive management, operational management, and staff of the organization; customers or consumers who will be affected by the services/products delivered; business partners and suppliers; other departments, divisions or offices; internal and/or external audit; compliance departments; security; health and safety; business continuity; trade unions; political or regulatory bodies;

the wider community in which the affected organization exists; and project and programme management teams delivering projects and programmes.

6.5.4 Provides clear guidance

Risk management for the operational perspective should be shaped by the risk management policy and process guide and is documented in the operational risk management strategy.

The risk management strategy for the operational perspective will define how risk management will be handled during the lifetime of the operational unit or service. In particular, it is used to show close links to security, health and safety, business continuity management and contingent plans.

6.5.5 Informs decision-making

Operational risk reporting is fundamental to an organization's understanding of its exposure to risks and how it is managing them. Operational management and independent personnel, such as those responsible for conducting internal and/or external audits, should conduct regular reviews against operational controls to ensure these controls are appropriate, complete and being adhered to.

Every member of staff within the organization should be responsible for reporting a breach in an internal control and identifying additional risks. These should be recorded and escalated to management for assessment, control and, if they exceed the risk tolerance levels, further escalation or notification to senior management. The management team should provide exception reports against the controls regularly and identify any additional risks and how they have been assessed and treated.

6.5.6 Facilitates continual improvement

For a new service, the risk management process should commence at the outset with the key risks captured as part of the concept identification. During subsequent definition, the full process should be applied with a key output being an operational risk management strategy that defines how the management of risk will be handled during the lifetime of the service. As risks are identified and assessed, this information will be captured in the operational risk register together with the planned risk responses once they are agreed.

At the end of each service review point, the operational risk management strategy should be reviewed for its effectiveness, lessons learned should be documented, and the full risk process should be repeated incorporating lessons learned from earlier iterations.

6.5.7 Creates a supportive culture

The operations manager has a key role to play in creating a supportive culture for risk management for their area. If the operations manager shows through words and actions that risk management is important, others will follow.

Glossary

accept
A risk response that means that the organization takes the chance that the risk will occur, with full impact on objectives if it does.

accounting officer
A public sector role. Has personal responsibility for the propriety and regularity of the finances for which he or she is answerable; for the keeping of proper accounts; for prudent and economical administration; for avoidance of waste and extravagance; and for the efficient and effective use of resources. This brings with it a responsibility for governance issues, and includes custodianship of risk management and its adoption throughout the organization.

avoid
A risk response that seeks to eliminate a threat by making the situation certain.

business continuity management
A holistic management process that identifies potential impacts that threaten an organization and provides a framework for building resilience with the capability for an effective response that safeguards the interests of its key stakeholders, reputation, brand and value-creating activities. The management of recovery or continuity in the event of a disaster. Also the management of the overall process through training, rehearsals and reviews, to ensure the business continuity plan stays current and up to date.

communications plan
A plan of the communications activities during the organizational activity (strategic, programme, project or operational) that will be established and maintained. Typically contains when, what, how and with whom information flows.

contingent plan
Plans intended for use, only if required, e.g. if a risk response is not successful. Often called fallback plans.

corporate governance
The ongoing activity of maintaining a sound system of internal control by which the directors and officers of an organization ensure that effective management systems, including financial monitoring and control systems, have been put in place to protect assets, earnings capacity and the reputation of the organization.

early warning indicator
Abbreviated to EWI. A leading indicator for an organizational objective measured ultimately by a key performance indicator (KPI).

enhance
A risk response for an opportunity that seeks to increase the probability and/or impact to make it more certain.

exploit
A risk response for an opportunity that seeks to make the uncertain situation certain.

fallback plan
See contingent plan.

impact
Impact is the result of a particular threat or opportunity actually occurring.

inherent risk
The exposure arising from a specific risk before any action has been taken to manage it.

issue
A relevant event that has happened, was not planned and requires management action. It could be a problem, benefit, query, concern, change request or risk that has occurred.

key performance indicator
Abbreviated to KPI. A measure of performance that is used to help an organization define and evaluate how successful it is in making progress towards its organizational objectives.

management of risk
Systematic application of policies, procedures, methods and practices to the tasks of identifying and assessing risks, and then planning and implementing risk responses. This provides a disciplined environment for proactive decision-making.

operational risk
Failure to achieve business/organizational objectives due to human error, system failures and/or inadequate procedure and controls.

opportunity
An uncertain event that would have a favourable impact on objectives or benefits if it occurred.

probability
This is the evaluated likelihood of a particular threat or opportunity actually happening, including a consideration of the frequency with which this may arise.

programme
A temporary, flexible organization structure created to coordinate, direct and oversee the implementation of a set of related projects and activities in order to deliver outcomes and benefits related to the organization's strategic objectives. A programme is likely to have a life that spans several years.

programme risk
Risk concerned with transforming high-level strategy into new ways of working to deliver benefits to the organization.

project
A temporary organization that is created for the purpose of delivering one or more business products according to a specified business case.

project risk
Project risks are those concerned with the successful completion of the project. Typically these risks include personal, technical, cost, schedule, resource, operational support, quality and supplier issues.

proximity
(of risk) The time factor of risk, i.e. the occurrence of risks will be due at particular times, and the severity of their impact will vary depending on when they occur.

reduce
A risk response for a threat that seeks to reduce probability and/or impact.

residual risk
The risk remaining after the risk response has been successfully applied.

risk
An uncertain event or set of events that, should it occur, will have an effect on the achievement of objectives. A risk is measured by a combination of the probability of a perceived threat or opportunity occurring and the magnitude of its impact on objectives.

risk actionee
Some actions may not be within the remit of the risk owner to control explicitly; in that situation there should be a nominated owner of the action to address the risk. He or she will need to keep the risk owner apprised of the situation.

risk appetite
The amount of risk the organization, or subset of it, is willing to accept.

risk capacity
The maximum amount of risk that an organization, or subset of it, can bear, linked to factors such as its reputation, capital, assets and ability to raise additional funds.

risk cause
A description of the source of the risk, i.e. the event or situation that gives rise to the risk.

risk effect
A description of the impact that the risk would have on the organizational activity should the risk materialize.

risk event
A description of the area of uncertainty in terms of the threat or the opportunity.

risk exposure
The extent of risk borne by the organization at that time.

risk management
Systematic application of principles, approach and processes to the tasks of identifying and assessing risks, and then planning and implementing risk responses.

risk management policy
A high-level statement showing how risk management will be handled throughout the organization.

risk management process guide
Describes the series of steps (from identify through to implement) and their respective associated activities, necessary to implement risk management.

risk management strategy
Describes the goals of applying risk management to the activity, the process that will be adopted, the roles and responsibilities, risk thresholds, the timing of risk management interventions, the deliverables, the tools and techniques that will be used, and the reporting requirements. It may also describe how the process will be coordinated with other management activities.

risk owner
A role or individual responsible for the management and control of all aspects of individual risks, including the implementation of the measures taken in respect of each risk.

risk profile
Describes the types of risk faced by an organization and its exposure to those risks.

risk register
A record of all identified risks relating to an initiative, including their status and history. Also called a risk log.

risk response
Actions that may be taken to bring the situation to a level where the exposure to risk is acceptable to the organization. These responses fall into one of a number of risk response options.

risk tolerance
The threshold levels of risk exposure that, with appropriate approvals, can be exceeded, but which when exceeded will trigger some form of response (e.g. reporting the situation to senior management for action).

senior responsible owner
The single individual with overall responsibility for ensuring that a project or programme meets its objectives and delivers the projected benefits.

share
A risk response. Modern procurement methods commonly entail a form of risk-sharing through the application of a pain/gain formula: both parties share the gain (within pre-agreed limits) if the cost is less than the cost plan; and share the pain (again within pre-agreed limits) if the cost plan is exceeded.

sponsor
The main driving force behind a programme or project.

stakeholder
Any individual, group or organization that can affect, be affected by, or perceive itself to be affected by, an initiative (programme, project, activity or risk).

strategic risk
Risk concerned with where the organization wants to go, how it plans to get there, and how it can ensure survival.

threat
An uncertain event that could have a negative impact on objectives or benefits.

transfer
A risk response whereby a third party takes on responsibility for an aspect of the risk.